Kindness Mindset in Leadership

Discover Why Kindness Matters for Effectiveness in Leadership

Ruby Taylor

© **Copyright 2023 - All rights reserved.**

The content contained within this book may not be reproduced, duplicated or transmitted without direct written permission from the author or the publisher.

Under no circumstances will any blame or legal responsibility be held against the publisher, or author, for any damages, reparation, or monetary loss due to the information contained within this book, either directly or indirectly.

Legal Notice:

This book is copyright protected. It is only for personal use. You cannot amend, distribute, sell, use, quote or paraphrase any part, or the content within this book, without the consent of the author or publisher.

Disclaimer Notice:

Please note the information contained within this document is for educational and entertainment purposes only. All effort has been executed to present accurate, up to date, reliable, complete information. No warranties of any kind are declared or implied. Readers acknowledge that the author is not engaged in the rendering of legal, financial, medical or professional advice. The content within this book has been derived from various sources. Please consult a licensed professional before attempting any techniques outlined in this book.

By reading this document, the reader agrees that under no circumstances is the author responsible for any losses, direct or indirect, that are incurred as a result of the use of the information contained within this document, including, but not limited to, errors, omissions, or inaccuracies.

Table of Contents

INTRODUCTION 1

CHAPTER 1: DEFINITION OF KINDNESS AND WHY IT MATTERS IN LEADERSHIP 3

CHAPTER 2: PERCEPTIONS OF KINDNESS 6

CHAPTER 3: CURRENT NEED FOR CHANGE 8

CHAPTER 4: THE MOST COMMON REASONS PEOPLE QUIT THEIR JOBS 10

CHAPTER 5: MINDSET CHANGE—A CULTURE OF KINDNESS .. 13

CHAPTER 6: BARRIERS TO KINDNESS 15

CHAPTER 7: FOCUSING ON KINDNESS 18

CHAPTER 8: THE POWER OF BEING POSITIVE 20

CHAPTER 9: ACTION STEPS FOR LEADERS (TIP SHEET) 22

CONCLUSION: THE FUTURE OF "KINDNESS MINDSET" IN LEADERSHIP 27

RESOURCES 29

Introduction

Leaders wear many hats and take on many challenges on a day-to-day basis, but all have a common desire to be successful in their roles. At any given time, the role changes from one situation to another, and you are leading people of many diverse backgrounds. Most leaders do not have training on the many diverse cultures that they lead or on their generational backgrounds. Leaders are new or experienced, and some are trying to figure out what defines them or how they are perceived by others. The answers are not always simple. There is usually more than one answer.

I have been in leadership positions for over thirty years, and although I am not the top expert, I can offer some knowledge that may be helpful to some. I have found that the simplest equation to success in leadership is kindness. Kindness is the umbrella that encompasses compassion, respect, genuineness, authenticity, humility, and positivity. You pretty much have to have those traits to be kind consistently and for it to be meaningful. No matter how hard a problem has been over the years, I've found that staying respectful and kind has helped the solution be at least honest and professional. Kindness helps you to be open to others' ideas, to listen without malice, and to take action without impeding others for win-win results. If you are unkind, none of the aforementioned can occur.

Kindness sounds easy in leadership. I have found that it is quite the opposite for some leaders. People perceive servant leaders as weak, pushovers, and unknowledgeable or uncredible if they behave in this manner. We all know tough leaders that get results but also cause fear and intimidation. Wouldn't it be great to be a leader that gets results without fear and intimidation? Many leaders do! However, there are far too many who don't. We see that in our high turnover and people not returning to their jobs, especially during the pandemic. They remember how they were treated, and it is not worth it to go back to the same environment. Life, as we knew it before, has become more precious, and our families have taken center stage. As leaders, we need to understand the new ways people interact with each other and how that means we need to lead with more compassion and kindness.

I'm excited to talk about some acts of kindness that have helped me get through difficult times and do well as a leader. In the following chapters, I will share some helpful examples to get through one day at a time in the role of leadership by leading with kindness.

Chapter 1:

Definition of Kindness and Why It Matters in Leadership

Let's start with the definition of kindness to make sure we are all on the same page.

Webster's Dictionary defines *kind* as "disposed to be good to others and make them happy by granting their request, supplying their wants, or assisting them in distress."

The Oxford Dictionary defines *kindness* as "a behavior marked by ethical characteristics, a pleasant disposition, and concern and consideration for others." In many cultures and religions, it is seen as a good thing and something of value.

The kindness trait of a leader is important in today's world. When it comes to leadership traits, one of the most important traits a leader should have is kindness. When people do kind things, hormones are released that make people feel less stressed and calm.

With many people on edge and worried about the present and future economies and other uncertainties, it is an asset to any organization to have leaders that display an aura of calmness and kindness. Because of their calm demeanor and ability to be positive and work out a collaborative solution, they have an advantage in preventing many situations from becoming volatile.

Synonyms for *kindness*:

- kindliness
- kindheartedness
- warm-heartedness
- goodwill
- affectionateness
- affection
- warmth
- gentleness
- tenderness
- concern
- care

Universally, we all know what it means to be kind to someone or what the act of being kind entails. Kindness may look different to some of us. Some may see kindness as just being polite or smiling, while others see it as going beyond politeness and providing a level of support or relief.

In leadership, kindness needs to go to a deeper level for sustainability and to gain trust by being genuine. Kindness is important for leaders to have because it's expensive for companies to train people over and over again, only to lose them after less than a year. Leader productivity is impacted in the process, as well, with this duplication process.

Most of this cost can be alleviated simply by changing the way we treat employees. Of course, it does not address 100% of turnover, but it will impact a significant amount. The days of being a tough leader are over. This style of leadership is too risky and close to aggressive behavior, harassment, and bullying of employees. This becomes an institutional risk to allow leaders to lead in this fashion. It matters to the organization as a whole.

Leadership training programs help organizations because they give leaders the tools they need to encourage kind behavior.

Leaders want to be successful, but to make sure they are, they need strong mentorship programs. We all need someone to talk through leadership situations with to make sure we are on the right track. We need someone to validate how we handle difficult situations, especially as new leaders. Hats off to most leaders because, for many, it was "baptism by fire," so to speak, and most did their best. Most of the toughness came from how they were led by other leaders or external factors.

Chapter 2:

Perceptions of Kindness

Let's start with what kindness is not. Kindness is not being a pushover or being weak as a leader. It does not mean you are not standing up for your convictions or what is right. It is actually a sign of your courage. For example, a leader that struggles with grammar may need a suggestion to take a series of short grammar classes that could be taken for practice to help improve writing skills.

This can be pointed out without making them feel bad about the errors they are making. This was shared once with a leader, and about three years later, she was thankful because no one ever told her. She later improved remarkably in this area. I think back and realize that some may think that being kind or nice is like saying nothing. However, kindness means caring about the other person and wanting to help them be successful.

Kindness is extending yourself on a much deeper level than politeness. As a leader, you are listening and observing to see what struggles your team members are having and seeing how you can help them, or talking to them to see what help they think they need.

The employee, in turn, feels that they have been acknowledged, and it is also an opportunity to build a foundation of trust.

You are a positive leader (guide) for your team who is nonjudgmental and noncontrolling. They need to feel that you care without feeling that someone is being condescending. You are already in a higher-level role, so there is nothing that needs to be proven. Kindness is the ability to be humble. If we are threatened in our role as leaders, we lead in that fashion. For example, we began to protect knowledge and information and not share it for our team to grow. It becomes a practice and an unconscious act before we realize it. The impact could affect efficiency and productivity. Kindness means leading with confidence and being happy with yourself to create a place where people of all levels can learn. Kindness is caring.

Kind leaders are sometimes seen as weak. People can easily exploit their weaknesses. The leader has to be careful that others don't practice taking authority over them, as this is typically what others do. They may also perceive them as boring and not smart enough for the job. People can sometimes perceive that you are okay with anything, and you get dumped with extra work because you are nice and won't say no. In all cases, there must be a balance to prevent being taken advantage of. *Kindness* means standing your ground and not being manipulated.

Chapter 3:

Current Need for Change

It is a known fact that leaders with traits of being tough, mean, and inflexible began to have some staff that functioned in the same fashion. There is also a risk of staff not sharing information openly to make sure the organization runs efficiently out of fear of being ridiculed or embarrassed by these types of leaders. This type of leadership is at risk for bullying-type behavior any time employees are in fear while trying to do their job. On the surface, an area may appear to be running smoothly but may have underlying problems. Unfortunately, leaders are told by some in upper management that "being soft" is a weakness in leadership and an area that they need to improve. In reality, it should be a leadership skill that is promoted for a better work environment.

Organizations also have students and interns that work in environments that we hope will come back and work, ideally. If they are in a place where kindness is not portrayed, it is unlikely that they will choose it as their place of employment. If they do, they may not stay very long. The cost of training employees is too high to take a chance on not taking all measures to keep them.

Organizations are charged with being highly reliable in all areas of customer service. In the book, *The Patient Comes Second*, a radical look at customer service showed that improving the way employees were treated improved customer service. This extends to how we treat employees as leaders, which can have an impact on the performance of our teams in any type of workplace, whether it's a hospital, grocery store, retail store, food industry, or other critical industry.

Employees seek guidance from leaders and expect to be treated with dignity, but also to know that even if rules apply to them, there is a form of compassion that takes place in decision-making.

Chapter 4:

The Most Common Reasons People Quit Their Jobs

We could all use a huge dose of kindness. Kindness is not just an add-on for the workplace or the right thing to do. Research has shown that kindness can create an edge for success and productivity in the workplace. The effects of the pandemic have been felt worldwide on employment and staffing needs.

Many did not return to work for various reasons. Although the work-life balance was one of the reasons, some people did not return due to poor treatment or unpleasant working conditions. The good news is that many leaders now have an opportunity to do a reset on leadership and adjust the strategies of training and curriculum education to incorporate acts of kindness and what it means to lead in this fashion by promoting the benefits.

Below is a look at the top reasons that people are leaving their jobs.

Employees choose to leave their job for many reasons, including those listed below:

- Unsatisfied with Management
- Little opportunity for growth
- Compensation

- Outdated techniques or products
- Lack of engagement
- Overworked
- No check-ins from leadership
- Lack of challenges
- Inflexibility in the workplace
- Core values are unclear
- Retaining toxic employees
- Little acknowledgment

From the list, we can see that several directly relate to leadership interaction with the employee and the way they were made to feel about something in particular. Some things, however, are beyond the leader's control.

Some of the reasons can be fixed faster than others. These include not being acknowledged, not being checked in on, not being happy with management, and not being involved. Some that are more system-wide would take longer to address. Leaders are able to review employee satisfaction survey results or take custom surveys to see where they stand and start making changes to make a difference. We want employees to enjoy coming to work every day, so it is critical that they work in environments where they feel calm and supported rather than stressed and unsupported. We may see less sick time being used as well.

Stress at work results in illnesses and subsequent time off. Many people struggled with the pandemic by making adjustments to childcare, work, school, and general finances.

The long-term impact still lingers for many. Mental health is also an issue that many are dealing with in life. Life is not the same for many of us. The workplace is where a lot of time is spent, and it is also where the effort for chaos should be reduced as much as possible. Workplace violence is a concern for many, and people are on edge, which makes leading with kindness more imperative for leaders. There is an enormous amount of employee stress and uncertainty at any given time.

Chapter 5:

Mindset Change—A Culture of Kindness

Being too soft and compassionate is an area for improvement for leaders who need to change or shift their paradigm. Kindness should be promoted as something we want to see in our leaders if we expect the culture to change in the way employees are treated. Research has shown that leaders who are kind-hearted also tend to be compassionate, respectful, trustworthy, and honest.

One question to ask: Are you kind to yourself? Maybe we need to start by being nicer to ourselves by being less critical and blaming ourselves. Part of changing our culture is changing the way we feel about ourselves and think of ourselves. There is more right with you than wrong with you. You help people more than you think. People look up to you and need you more than you think. Focus on your positive traits and enhance them. They make you unstoppable.

Leaders in the workplace can use a culture of kindness strategies as a way to make changes.

Here are 4 Formats that can be utilized:
1. **Inspirational platform**: A kindness campaign can be constructed to inspire staff to rally kindness initiatives

as a group/team. Kindness Champions can be utilized much like other initiatives and projects.

2. **Promote behaviors of kindness**: Leaders can collaborate with Human Relations and/or Employee Experience Departments to devise creative ways to encourage and reward acts of kindness that stand out.

3. **Leadership prerequisite**: A shift from the old style of grit and toughness of a leader that is willing to sacrifice anyone or blame others to get results or not be accountable for results is outdated. Leaders should be supported and a prerequisite for hiring should be their ability to connect and be compassionate with staff.

4. **Practice**: The workplace can be transformed by these behaviors that start with leaders for role modeling and staff accountability for long term stability. The act of implementing moments of thoughtfulness and acts of kindness goes a long way for positive outcomes throughout all departments and operations.

Chapter 6:

Barriers to Kindness

Many reasons come to mind when you think of what may keep a leader from being kind, and here are a few that have been shared:

1. I may be seen as a weak or soft leader.
2. Too busy today.
3. I am already polite.
4. I already have good manners.
5. I fear rejection if I reach out.
6. Tired.
7. Misinterpretation.
8. Invading privacy.
9. Embarrassment.
10. Too stressed to add more to my plate.
11. Shy.
12. I'll wait for next time.

13. I am already hurting or angry about something.

14. No one is kind to me on a regular basis.

15. I was kind last week.

Kindness is a reflection of when you step out of your comfort zone and check in on someone else to make them feel better. Surprisingly, when you do, it also makes *you* feel better. This is because kindness has a boomerang effect.

The kindness you give comes back to you. You have taken a step toward changing the world by reaching out and connecting to that one person who continues the connection with someone else, in most cases.

Many times, leaders overthink a situation and do not reach out to help someone because they are afraid of invading their privacy, even though the other person may need someone to listen to them or engage with them. There may be a fear that they will tell you too much, and you will become burdened and unable to assist. It's okay to let go of the fear and be supportive since, in most cases, people are not seeking advice. They usually want to vent to de-stress. You may only have to listen with compassion. You may prevent someone from contemplating self-harm. We never know what burdens people are carrying.

They sometimes seek acknowledgment that someone knows they are going through a rough time but still coming to work and doing a good job. Notifying you (their leader) may provide them with relief when you reach out and relieve their stress so they can get through the day. It shows empathy.

Kindness may become a journey, but it is important to just get started with implementing acts of kindness. Enjoy where you are and move forward to reap the benefits, as there will be many at work and in life. There are many perceptions, and it doesn't matter how many there are as long as you are true to yourself and meet people where they are with respect and kindness.

Keep in mind that many people are suffering inside at any given time. Words that work are words that elevate and make others feel special and important. People basically want to be heard and feel like their ideas matter. As a leader, you can break down barriers that you might put up by accident. It's time to take an inventory of where you stand for self-awareness. It's time to be accountable because that is really self-care.

Chapter 7:

Focusing On Kindness

Wherever we are as leaders on our journey toward a mindset of kindness, there is room for improvement or a time to help other leaders on their journey. Some tend to dismiss people who are optimistic in the wake of problems. Optimism does not mean you are not being realistic, that there is a problem at hand, or that you are ignoring it. Optimism is a form of determination to focus on the best outcome and work to make it a reality.

People will migrate to you when you are a positive leader. They are looking for someone who is optimistic, rather than someone who is pessimistic, which makes them fearful and anxious. The workplace can sometimes be in crisis mode, depending on where you work. One crisis after another can wear on anyone. Being supportive and kind offers a relief valve or outlet. A kind word can suffice when nothing else can.

Kindness gives us the opportunity to live in the moment. Today is full of complex, busy schedules being juggled. Many are looking at the past and worrying about the future while trying to balance everything in the middle. The act of kindness allows us to experience what we have in front of us—the present. Kindness is teachable and can be practiced by anyone.

It is a conscious effort that a leader can make and decide to do, as far as taking certain measures to practice or change a current practice to improve upon it.

When a leader focuses on kindness, they focus on doing good for someone else and making a connection with that person in their current environment. The advantage is that they also feel good. The connection goes on to impact a community. You are able to give something outside of yourself.

It is a selfless act of humility when you offer yourself in an act of kindness. As you elevate others, you elevate yourself. The act of giving kindness creates a ripple effect in the universe. Many have heard of the Law of Attraction.

It is simply that the positive mannerisms that you send out have a way of coming back to you. Being positive is a way to channel your energy, and you can choose to be negative or positive. Being negative has many untoward effects on your health and how you see life in general.

Self-care is important for every leader if they want to be able to lead in today's challenging, constantly changing, and fast-paced environment. The flow of positive energy will help sustain success when all else fails.

Most of the fortitude for leadership survival will come from within, and that will be a kindness to yourself and to others. You can depend on it to be unwavering. It will be your go-to way to get out of sticky situations quickly and confidently while commanding respect. It will be easier to negotiate and collaborate in a supportive environment. Start with kindness and end with kindness in your conversations. Also, this should be the way you start and end your day. There is no need to take negativity home or bring it to work. Kickstart your day with kindness.

Chapter 8:

The Power of Being Positive

Positive self-talk is a great tool for any leader to help maintain a positive state of mind. It would be a challenge to conduct acts of kindness without a positive state of mind. In most cases, you must use self-help skills and be your own cheerleader by loving and believing in yourself. You want to be the kind of leader that is approachable, not one that people want to avoid. Begin by being positive toward yourself in order to be positive toward others. It will become an important part of your self-image and your life.

Become a leader with what you hope to give: kindness, joy, hope, and encouragement. Our ultimate goal as a leader should be to inspire others. Be the kind of leader that others want to follow and want to be around. If you are being negative, not only are you draining yourself, but you are draining everyone around you, including your family and friends. You can use that energy to be kinder. Being kind is much easier and less stressful.

Being positive goes beyond smiling. Being positive is a state of mind with specific actions that we must take to be in a certain frame of mind. I choose to use positive affirmations to start and end the day.

Also, during the day, I use affirmations. When things get tough, I've discovered that you have to be your own cheerleader because other people may not always have your best interests in mind. In addition, people are busy and don't have time to support your issues. In some cases, you have to deal with naysayers. Stay positive and keep moving forward by scripting five affirmations that you will say when the going gets tough.

Here are a few to share that you can tweak to personalize or totally redo:

The first one is considered one of the most powerful affirmations to start the day with and contains only five powerful words. If you only had time for one, that could be the only one required.

I intend to feel good.

Other affirmations used are the following:
- I love helping others.
- I never give up.
- I am grateful for all opportunities to learn.
- I am grateful.
- I am worthy.
- I am loved.
- I am positive.
- I am where I need to be, and all is alright with the world.
- It's all good.
- Good things are coming my way!

Chapter 9:

Action Steps for Leaders (Tip Sheet)

Here are some suggestions to get you off to a good start for kindness activities for you or your teams:

1. Find a *Kindness Partner*: For starters, you will be able to hold each other accountable for being kind to one another for starters. You can also discuss new measures you have adopted with your teams.

2. Form a *Kindness Committee*: Discuss with your leadership the team measures you will take to show acts of kindness towards your employees related to their well-being, acknowledgment, and making them feel good at work.

3. Establish a weekly and/or monthly *Kindness Award*.

4. Pick a *Connect Day* and get to know 1–2 staff members. It can be something personal that they want to share about themselves, their children, or a family member.

5. Find out an immediate team member's favorite cookie, candy bar, or drink(juice/soda) and leave it on their desk for a birthday or any day for a surprise. A thank-

you note can also be added as an opportunity to thank them for the great job they have done.

6. Create an individual development plan (IDP) to determine what your immediate team needs to support them. They may want to be a better speaker, improve their computer skills, improve their writing skills, or receive other training. It can be used to track their staff development and ensure you are having engaging conversations.

7. Set up a "Go Do Acts of Kindness Day" for your team with details of each doing a kind act for the other with their input.

8. Frequently, teams conduct daily or weekly huddle reporting. Kindness can be added as an agenda item or topic for quick discussion, updates or acknowledgement.

9. If you walk by one of your employees, make eye contact, say "hello," and smile. Normally, if you walk by a piece of furniture, you don't do anything, but they are not a piece of furniture. It's a basic form of acknowledgment, and they will remember that you acknowledged them. Actually, this is more commonly voiced by employees than you may be aware of.

10. When you enter a room with your employees, always make an effort to speak to all when feasible. Staff feel ignored when you only speak to a select few. Be kind and say hello to all that you lead. This will also avoid allegations of favoritism or lack of inclusion in other matters of leadership.

11. Give honest compliments generously. However, they must be genuine. Notice the best in people and let them know. People welcome feedback or praise about themselves. Remember that staff should not have to wait once a year to hear how they are performing during an appraisal. A compliment can go a long way toward validating them and making them feel like the leadership cares about them or that the work they do is important.

12. Practice gratitude. You can never say "thank you" too many times when you genuinely mean it.

13. Acknowledgments: Send group and/or individual emails to celebrate birthdays, work anniversaries, certifications, and degrees. It will show you care, so take the time to do them by setting calendar reminders at the beginning of each year, as feasible. Make it a priority for new staff dates to be added to your calendar that frequently gets overlooked.

14. Avoid having any one employee spend too much time in your office or with you. Others see this as favoritism and feel left out. Kindness is making sure others feel included.

15. Follow the policy for scheduling, time, and attendance in an equitable fashion to prevent feelings of favoritism. Kindness is treating everyone fairly that you lead in order to gain trust in the workplace, not only towards you but also to maintain high morale among each team member. Avoid causing animosity among your team through your own actions.

16. Smile and be friendly as much as feasible to create a positive environment and calm the negativity. People have a hard time being negative when you are smiling. There is enough to frown about, so lighten up and stop looking so serious about the smallest things. Think of a joke or funny story to tell every now and then to share with others. Make someone chuckle. Laughter really is still the best medicine!

17. Fun Activities: Reach out to your Human Relations (HR) or Employee Experience Department to partner with for team building exercises; allow the team to decide how they would like to have fun or share ideas they have as well.

When you display kindness, it is a sign of courage when you choose to speak calmly and avoid yelling or raising your voice in spite of others around you yelling or raising their voice. The benefits are that you maintain professionalism and poise among your employees and colleagues. You also avoid feelings of fear and anxiety. If you are being condescending too, it has the same impact as yelling. Change the way you make one person feel, and you will change how many feel. If you are meeting with one employee, that one employee may share with others how you handled a situation with them if you yell or are condescending.

Try to be kind and talk through a situation instead. Allow the employee to offer suggestions. Many times, as leaders, we talk more than is necessary.

We really can benefit from listening more and guiding staff. Allow them to figure out the fundamental solutions to a problem because that is when they will take responsibility for better results. When meeting with an employee, always plan to talk less, as this will make you appear more engaged. I have talked with many employees who felt like they were not able to get their point across or a word in when meeting with their leader. Their response was to shut down and leave, feeling worse with the problem unresolved. As leaders, we mean no harm because we have so much to say and want to help.

We show kindness by listening. There is a time to be silent and talk less. You will be seen as a confident and comfortable leader. The goal is to work on achieving leadership balance. Each situation or conversation changes by the minute and can go south quickly. You are less likely to escalate anxiety during a crucial conversation if you allow an employee to talk through what they have to say.

If you get off track, you can refocus or resume your topic of discussion to get back on track.

Conclusion:

The Future of "Kindness Mindset" in Leadership

Businesses will be more successful in the future if they embrace kindness formats and training platforms. Kindness initiatives have been shown to improve employee well-being by lowering anxiety and stress. Kindness measures have also helped leaders build trust in their teams, which in turn builds trust in the organization for better overall outcomes. Productivity improves, and turnover decreases. Kindness is simply the feeling that someone cares for you. No one wants to feel badly or be made to feel bad or sad. We all want to feel valued. If you are not cared for, you may feel alone. Leaders have the ability to be conscious of their acts of kindness. This is a choice we make at any given moment to be kind, and many times it costs us nothing to be kind. However, the time spent recovering from and repairing an unkind situation is time-consuming. Kindness comes back to us tenfold and is passed on over and over again from employee to employee.

The incorporation of a kind mindset into school curricula would benefit students studying the importance of leadership in business, nursing, economics, government policy, social services, and administration programs where leadership is part of the curriculum. Expectations and training should not be limited to the workplace; they should be integrated into all aspects of our education and training. The benefit will be that these new leaders will change the way people work and start kindness mindset programs to help employees and in turn benefit and help customers. This will lead to great results that will help our communities as a whole.

Go forward and lead with a *Kindness Mindset* and change your workplace with one kind act at a time. Your positive disposition and kind words have the power to turn someone's life around.

If you found this book helpful, I'd be very grateful if you left a favorable review for the book on Amazon! Thank you.

Resources

Baker, W., & O'Malley, M. (2008). *Leading with Kindness: How Good People Consistently Get Superior Results.* AMACOM.

Bankert. A. (2020). *Your Hidden Superpower: The Kindness That Makes You Unbeatable at Work and Connects You with Anyone.* Harper Collins Leadership.

Cameron, D. (2018). *A Year of Living Kindly: Choices That Will Change Your Life and the World Around You.* She Writes Press.

Gullixson, H. (2021). *Culture of Kindness At Work: Acts Of Kindness That Make Work More Enjoyable: Simple Acts Of Kindness At Work.* Independent.

Haskins, G., Thomas, G. & Lalit, J. (2018). *Kindness in Leadership.* Routledge Taylor & Francis Group.

Logothetis, L. (2019). *Go Be Kind: 28 ½ Adventures Guaranteed to Make You Happier* (1st ed.). Routledge.

Spiegelman, P. & Berrett, B. (2018). *Patients Come Second: Leading Change by Changing the Way You Lead.* Inc. Original.

Summers, N., & Che DI, L.P. (2019). *A Culture of Kindness: For the Leaders of the future.* Independently published.

Milton Keynes UK
Ingram Content Group UK Ltd.
UKHW011827151223
434437UK00007B/345